Harry Potter

MOVIE POSTER BOOK

VILLAINS

ISBN 978-0-545-23765-9

12 11 10 9 8 7 6 5 4 3 2 1   10 11 12 13 14 15/0
Printed in the U.S.A. First printing, October 2010   40

SCHOLASTIC INC.
NEW YORK TORONTO LONDON AUCKLAND
SYDNEY MEXICO CITY NEW DELHI HONG KONG

LORD VOLDEMORT™

EXTRA FACT:
KNOWN AS "HE-WHO-MUST-NOT-BE-NAMED" AND "THE HEIR OF SLYTHERIN"

LORD
VOLDEMORT™

TOM
MARVOLO
RIDDLE™

HOUSE:
SLYTHERIN

EXTRA FACT:
BECAME LORD VOLDEMORT

TOM MARVOLO RIDDLE™

BELLATRIX LESTRANGE™

FAMILY:

SIRIUS BLACK AND NYMPHADORA TONKS (COUSINS)
AND NARCISSA MALFOY (SISTER)

EXTRA FACTS:

DEATH EATER; MURDERED SIRIUS BLACK

PETER PETTIGREW™

EXTRA FACTS:
DEATH EATER; KNOWN AS "WORMTAIL"

PETER PETTIGREW

BARTY CROUCH, JR.

EXTRA FACTS:
DEATH EATER; IMPERSONATED MAD-EYE MOODY
DURING HARRY'S FOURTH YEAR AT HOGWARTS

BARTY CROUCH, JR.

ALBERT RUNCORN

EXTRA FACT:

MINISTRY EMPLOYEE INTO WHOM HARRY POTTER
TRANSFORMS USING POLYJUICE POTION

SCABIOR

EXTRA FACT:
SNATCHER ALONGSIDE FENRIR GREYBACK

LUCIUS MALFOY™

FAMILY:

NARCISSA MALFOY (WIFE) AND DRACO MALFOY (SON)

EXTRA FACTS:

DEATH EATER; SLIPPED TOM RIDDLE'S DIARY
INTO GINNY WEASLEY'S CAULDRON DURING
HER FIRST YEAR AT HOGWARTS

LUCIUS MALFOY™

NARCISSA MALFOY™

FAMILY:
LUCIUS MALFOY (HUSBAND), DRACO MALFOY (SON)
AND BELLATRIX LESTRANGE (SISTER)

EXTRA FACTS:
FORMED AN UNBREAKABLE VOW WITH SEVERUS SNAPE

NARCISSA MALFOY™

DRACO MALFOY™

HOUSE:
SLYTHERIN

FAMILY:
LUCIUS AND NARCISSA MALFOY (PARENTS)

EXTRA FACT:
DEATH EATER

DRACO MALFOY™

VINCENT CRABBE

GREGORY GOYLE

HOUSE:
SLYTHERIN

EXTRA FACT:
CRONIES OF DRACO MALFOY

PANSY PARKINSON

HOUSE:
SLYTHERIN

EXTRA FACT:
DATED DRACO MALFOY

FENRIR GREYBACK™

EXTRA FACTS:
WEREWOLF; DEATH EATER; SNATCHER

FENRIR GREYBACK™

DOLORES UMBRIDGE™

EXTRA FACTS:
SENIOR UNDER-SECRETARY TO THE MINISTER OF MAGIC; DEFENSE AGAINST THE DARK ARTS TEACHER DURING HARRY'S FIFTH YEAR; LATER, HEAD OF THE MUGGLE-BORN REGISTRATION COMMISSION

DOLORES UMBRIDGE™

VERNON DURSLEY

FAMILY:
PETUNIA (WIFE), DUDLEY (SON) AND HARRY POTTER (NEPHEW)

PETUNIA DURSLEY

FAMILY:
VERNON (HUSBAND), DUDLEY (SON) AND HARRY POTTER (NEPHEW)

DUDLEY DURSLEY

FAMILY:

PETUNIA AND VERNON (PARENTS)
AND HARRY POTTER (COUSIN)

DUDLEY
DURSLEY

NAGINI

LORD VOLDEMORT'S PET SNAKE
IS ALSO A HORCRUX

ARAGOG

ONCE HAGRID'S PET, THIS ACROMANTULA
LIVES IN THE FORBIDDEN FOREST

BASILISK

THIS BASILISK LIVED IN THE
CHAMBER OF SECRETS
AND WAS RELEASED BY THE
HEIR OF SLYTHERIN IN AN
ATTEMPT TO KILL MUGGLE-BORN
STUDENTS AT HOGWARTS

SEVERUS SNAPE™

PATRONUS:

DOE

EXTRA FACTS:

POTIONS MASTER DURING HARRY'S FIRST FIVE YEARS AT HOGWARTS;
DEFENSE AGAINST THE DARK ARTS TEACHER DURING HARRY'S SIXTH YEAR AT HOGWARTS;
HEADMASTER OF HOGWARTS AFTER HARRY LEAVES SCHOOL

SEVERUS SNAPE™

SEVERUS SNAPE ™

PATRONUS: DOE

EXTRA FACTS:
POTIONS MASTER DURING HARRY'S FIRST FIVE YEARS AT HOGWARTS;
DEFENSE AGAINST THE DARK ARTS TEACHER DURING HARRY'S SIXTH YEAR AT HOGWARTS;
HEADMASTER OF HOGWARTS AFTER HARRY LEAVES SCHOOL

BUCKBEAK TM
BUCKBEAK THE HIPPOGRIFF PLAYED A CRUCIAL ROLE IN GETTING SIRIUS BLACK TO SAFETY DURING HARRY'S THIRD YEAR AT HOGWARTS

CROOKSHANKS TM
HERMIONE'S CAT DETECTED SOMETHING ODD ABOUT RON'S RAT SCABBERS DURING THEIR THIRD YEAR AT HOGWARTS

HEDWIG TM
HARRY POTTER'S OWL, HEDWIG, WAS GIVEN TO HIM ON HIS ELEVENTH BIRTHDAY BY RUBEUS HAGRID

FAWKES TM
DUMBLEDORE'S PHOENIX, FAWKES, PROVIDED THE CORE FEATHER FOR EACH OF HARRY'S AND VOLDEMORT'S WANDS

KREACHER ™

EXTRA FACT:
HOUSE-ELF TO THE BLACK FAMILY
AND LATER TO HARRY POTTER

GRIPHOOK

RACE:
GOBLIN

EXTRA FACT:
GRINGOTTS BANK EMPLOYEE

DOBBY ™

EXTRA FACT:
HOUSE-ELF TO THE MALFOY FAMILY
BEFORE BEING ACCIDENTALLY
FREED BY LUCIUS MALFOY

ORDER OF
THE PHOENIX

CREATED BY ALBUS DUMBLEDORE TO FIGHT LORD VOLDEMORT

ALASTOR "MAD-EYE" MOODY

EXTRA FACTS:

AUROR; MEMBER OF THE ORDER OF THE PHOENIX; DEFENSE AGAINST THE DARK ARTS TEACHER DURING HARRY'S FOURTH YEAR AT HOGWARTS; HAS A MAGICAL EYE AND A WOODEN LEG

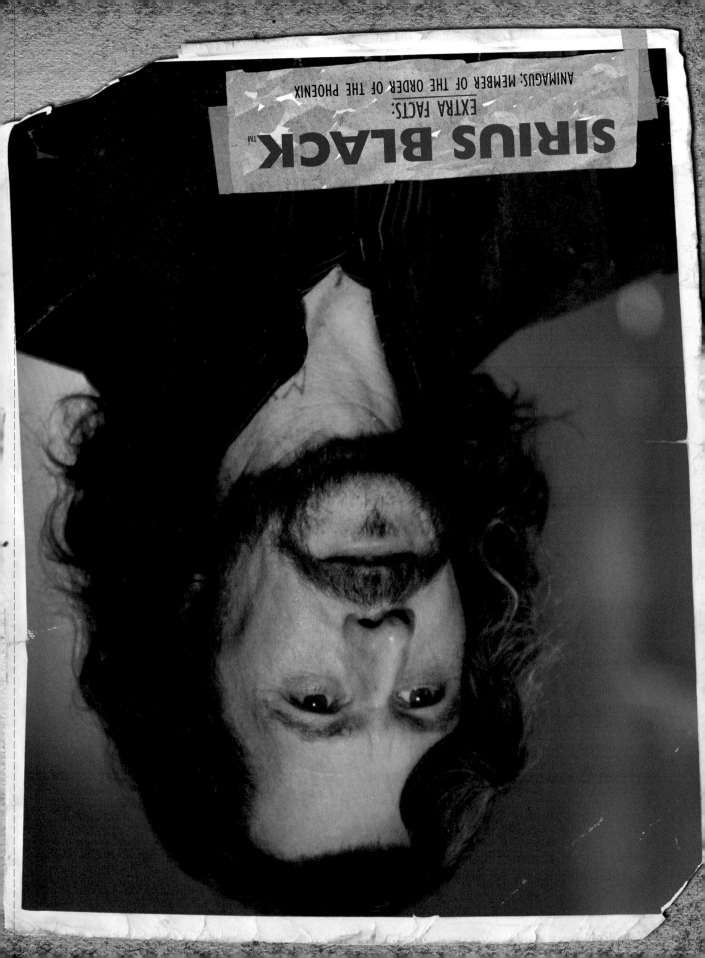

SIRIUS BLACK ™

EXTRA FACTS:
ANIMAGUS; MEMBER OF THE ORDER OF THE PHOENIX

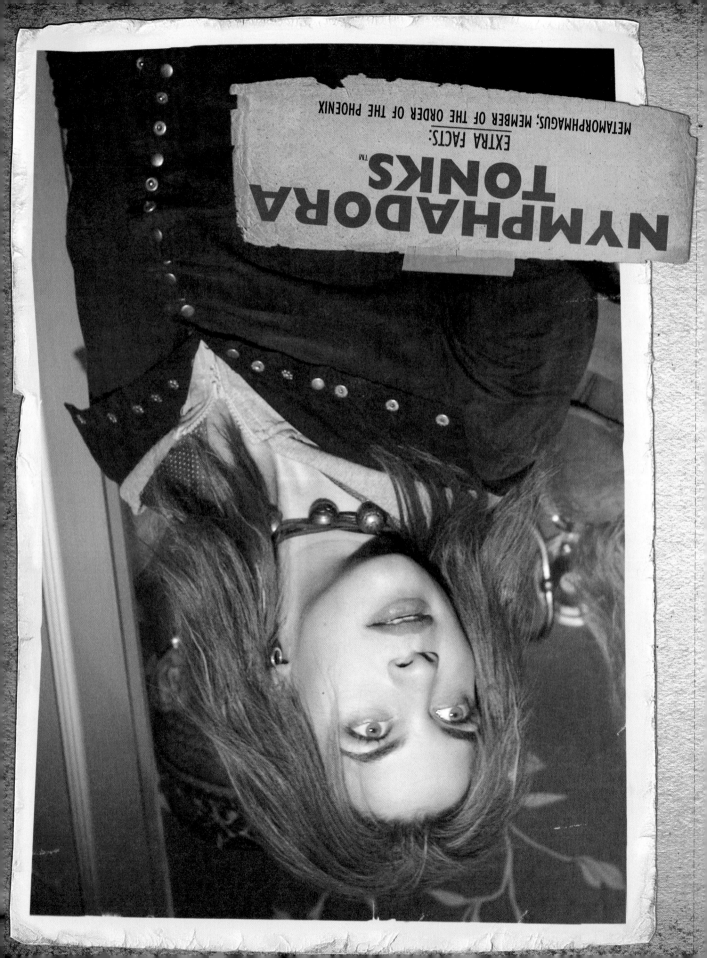

NYMPHADORA TONKS ™

EXTRA FACTS:
METAMORPHMAGUS; MEMBER OF THE ORDER OF THE PHOENIX

REMUS LUPIN™

EXTRA FACTS:
WEREWOLF; DEFENSE AGAINST THE DARK ARTS TEACHER
DURING HARRY'S THIRD YEAR AT HOGWARTS

ARTHUR WEASLEY

EXTRA FACTS:

WORKS IN THE MISUSE OF MUGGLE ARTIFACTS OFFICE IN THE MINISTRY OF MAGIC;
MEMBER OF THE ORDER OF THE PHOENIX

MOLLY WEASLEY

EXTRA FACT:
MEMBER OF THE ORDER OF THE PHOENIX

ABERFORTH DUMBLEDORE

EXTRA FACTS:
BARMAN AT THE HOG'S HEAD:
ALBUS DUMBLEDORE'S BROTHER

RUBEUS HAGRID ™

EXTRA FACTS:
KEEPER OF KEYS AND GROUNDS;
CARE OF MAGICAL CREATURES TEACHER AT HOGWARTS

MINERVA MCGONAGALL™

HOUSE: GRYFFINDOR
TEACHES: TRANSFIGURATION

POMONA SPROUT

HOUSE: HUFFLEPUFF
TEACHES: HERBOLOGY

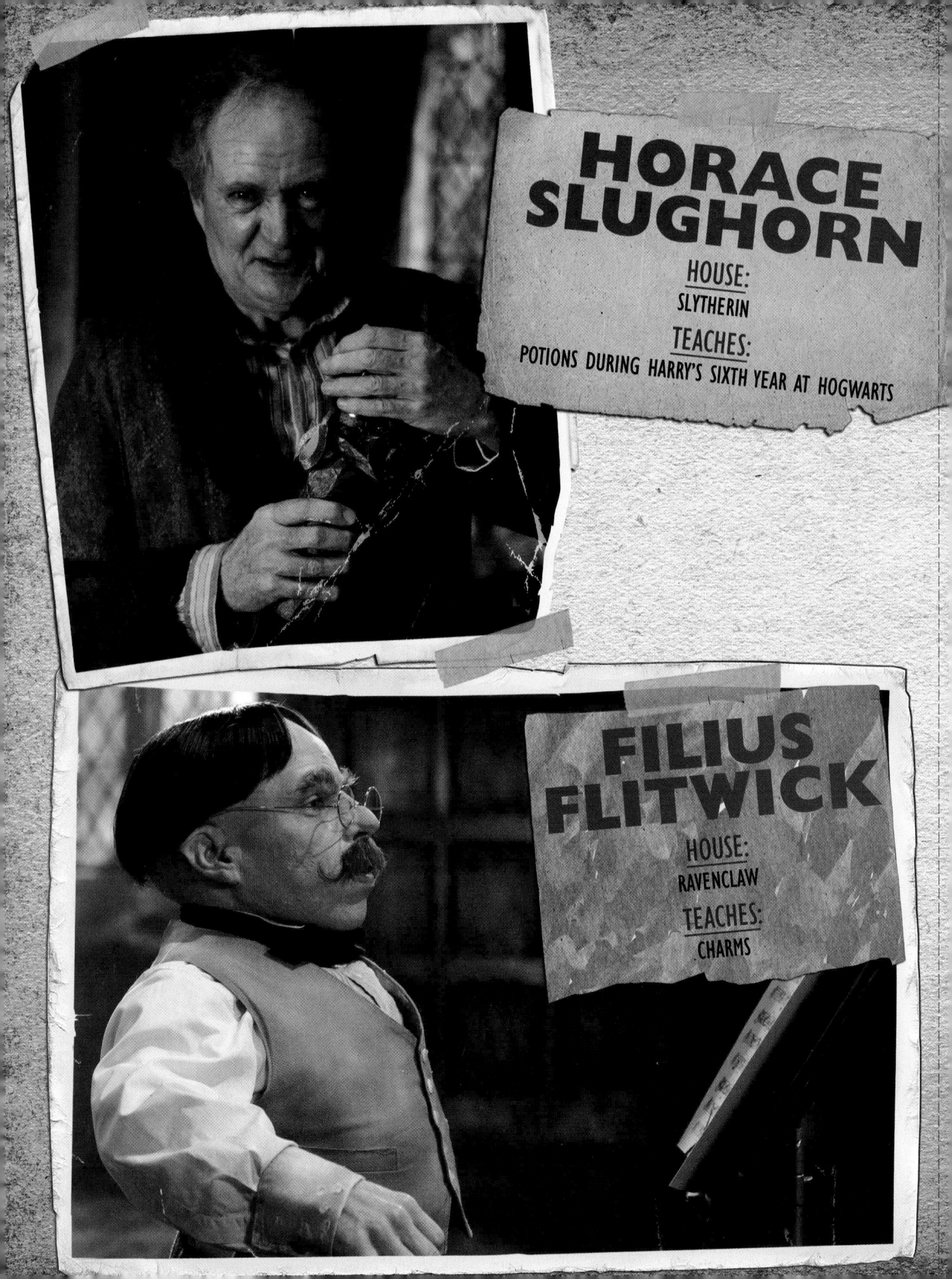

HORACE SLUGHORN

HOUSE:
SLYTHERIN

TEACHES:
POTIONS DURING HARRY'S SIXTH YEAR AT HOGWARTS

FILIUS FLITWICK

HOUSE:
RAVENCLAW

TEACHES:
CHARMS

ALBUS DUMBLEDORE

ALBUS
DUMBLEDORE™

PATRONUS: PHOENIX
EXTRA FACTS:
HEADMASTER OF HOGWARTS:
FOUNDER OF THE ORDER OF THE PHOENIX

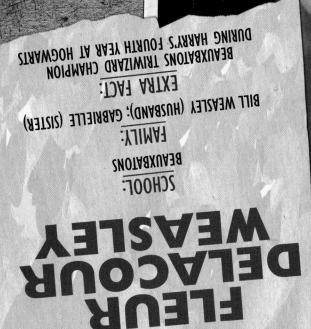

FLEUR DELACOUR WEASLEY

SCHOOL:
BEAUXBATONS

FAMILY:
BILL WEASLEY (HUSBAND); GABRIELLE (SISTER)

EXTRA FACT:
BEAUXBATONS TRIWIZARD CHAMPION
DURING HARRY'S FOURTH YEAR AT HOGWARTS

BILL WEASLEY

HOUSE:
GRYFFINDOR

FAMILY:
ARTHUR AND MOLLY (PARENTS); CHARLIE, BILL, PERCY, RON
AND GINNY WEASLEY (SIBLINGS); FLEUR DELACOUR (WIFE)

EXTRA FACT:
BITTEN BY FENRIR GREYBACK

FRED AND GEORGE WEASLEY

HOUSE:
GRYFFINDOR

FAMILY:
FRED AND GEORGE ARE TWINS;
ARTHUR AND MOLLY (PARENTS);
CHARLIE, BILL, PERCY, RON,
AND GINNY WEASLEY (SIBLINGS)

EXTRA FACT:
OWNERS OF WEASLEYS' WIZARD WHEEZES

CHO CHANG
HOUSE: RAVENCLAW

SEAMUS FINNIGAN
HOUSE: GRYFFINDOR

COLIN CREEVEY
HOUSE: GRYFFINDOR

PADMA PATIL
HOUSE: RAVENCLAW

LAVENDER BROWN
HOUSE: GRYFFINDOR

PARVATI PATIL
HOUSE: GRYFFINDOR

DUMBLEDORE'S ARMY ™

LUNA LOVEGOOD™

HOUSE:
RAVENCLAW

FAMILY:
XENOPHILIUS LOVEGOOD (FATHER)

PATRONUS:
HARE

EXTRA FACT:
FATHER IS EDITOR OF THE QUIBBLER

GINNY WEASLEY ™

HOUSE:
GRYFFINDOR

FAMILY:
ARTHUR AND MOLLY (PARENTS);
CHARLIE, BILL, PERCY, FRED, GEORGE
AND RON WEASLEY (BROTHERS)

HOBBY/INTEREST:
QUIDDITCH

EXTRA FACT:
POSSESSED BY VOLDEMORT
DURING HER FIRST YEAR AT HOGWARTS

NEVILLE LONGBOTTOM

NEVILLE LONGBOTTOM™

HOUSE: GRYFFINDOR

FAMILY: ALICE AND FRANK LONGBOTTOM (PARENTS)

HOBBY/INTEREST: HERBOLOGY

EXTRA FACT: LIVES WITH HIS GRANDMOTHER

HERMIONE GRANGER

HERMIONE GRANGER™

HOUSE:
GRYFFINDOR

PATRONUS:
OTTER

FAMILY:
MUGGLE-BORN, PARENTS ARE DENTISTS

HOBBY/INTEREST:
READING

EXTRA FACT:
TOP OF HER CLASS

RON WEASLEY™

HOUSE:
GRYFFINDOR

PATRONUS:
DOG

FAMILY:
ARTHUR AND MOLLY (PARENTS);
CHARLIE, BILL, PERCY, FRED, GEORGE
AND GINNY WEASLEY (SIBLINGS)

HOBBY/INTEREST:
WIZARD CHESS

EXTRA FACT:
TERRIFIED OF SPIDERS

RON
WEASLEY™

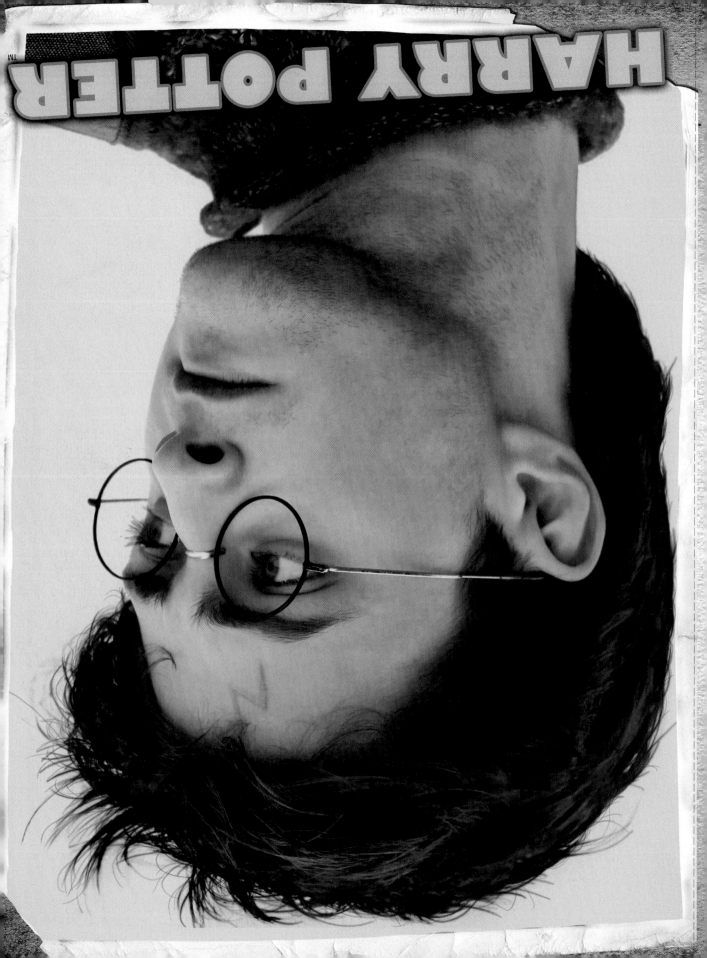

HARRY POTTER™

HOUSE: GRYFFINDOR

PATRONUS: STAG

FAMILY: LILY AND JAMES POTTER (PARENTS)

HOBBY/INTEREST: QUIDDITCH™

EXTRA FACT: KNOWN AS "THE BOY WHO LIVED" AND "THE CHOSEN ONE."

MOVIE POSTER BOOK

ISBN 978-0-545-23765-9

12 11 10 9 8 7 6 5 4 3 2 1   10 11 12 13 14 15/0
Printed in the U.S.A. First printing, October 2010   40

SCHOLASTIC INC.
NEW YORK TORONTO LONDON AUCKLAND
SYDNEY MEXICO CITY NEW DELHI HONG KONG